The Suitcase

by Sally Farrell Odgers   Illustrated by Margaret Power

The suitcase was the only thing she had, now. It was an old, brown one with cracks across the top and scuff marks on the corners. For as long as she could remember, it had been at the top of the cupboard, above the sheets and towels, where her mother had kept the spare blankets.

She had been panicking, trying to reach for the blankets, when it had happened. She had overbalanced and fallen, pulling the suitcase down on top of herself and breaking the rickety cane chair on which she had been standing.

She rubbed the bruise on her shoulder, and crouched down on the floor of the barn. Maybe it had been a bad idea to take the suitcase, but there had been no time to think or plan. Anyway, there was no way back now. They would have over-run the house, and the garden would be full of armed guards.

Amber paused at that moment to consider. Maybe "armed guards" was going a bit too far. She'd have to make it just two sentries instead. Or perhaps *four* sentries, one for each door and two at the gate. As for who *they* were, she'd worry about that later. For now, "they" could stand for all the invaders that had ever invaded anywhere. "The universal invader," said Amber aloud, and smiled. It sounded impressive. She wriggled into a more comfortable position and began a new page.

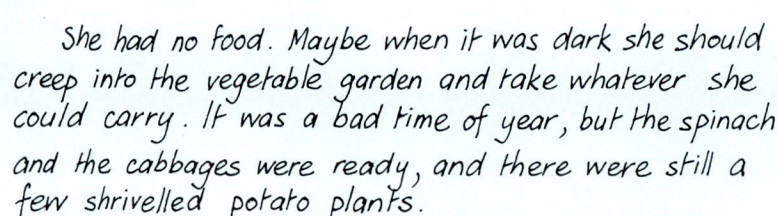

She had no food. Maybe when it was dark she should creep into the vegetable garden and take whatever she could carry. It was a bad time of year, but the spinach and the cabbages were ready, and there were still a few shrivelled potato plants.

Amber pulled a face at the idea of raw potatoes and spinach, but surely no fugitive would risk lighting a fire so close to the enemy, particularly in a barn. Come to think of it, a barn wouldn't be a good place to hide in at all. Sighing, Amber gave her barn a closed door and massive bolts.

But how hungry would you have to be to eat raw spinach? How about making it summer instead of winter? Then there would be carrots and strawberries and lettuce and things like that. Apples, even. Amber took a bite from the apple she had brought with her, and crunched reflectively. She shook her head. No, it shouldn't be in summer. This was going to be a cold, bleak story, and the time of year ought to fit in with that.

Shivering, she blew on her purple knuckles and unlatched the case, prying up the lid with her broken fingernails. It grated as it came free, and she glanced convulsively over her shoulder, shaking now with terror as well as cold. Would that small noise bring <u>them</u> into the barn? There was a long minute of suspense.

Amber read over what she had just written, and snorted. She could just hear her teacher's comments on that! "And what, Amber Dale, is a long minute? A minute with seventy seconds instead of sixty?" Amber thought. How about "moment"? A moment wasn't of any set length, was it? That'd do.

> the barn? There was a long ~~minute~~ moment of suspense. Her straining ears caught nothing but her own fluttering heartbeats. Gently, she tugged the case through the rustling hay to where a faint patch of winter sunlight straggled through the window.

Amber shook her head crossly. Of course barns didn't have windows! But she liked the idea of the little patch of light too much to let it go. So make it a stable instead. She scribbled a note in the margin, telling herself to go back and substitute the word "stable" for "barn" wherever it appeared in the story.

> The wan light made her skin look pale as parchment and she noticed that her hands were trembling as she lifted the lid. Disappointment came in a shattering rush as she stared at the small store of items she had rescued from the doomed house.

Amber crossed out the last three words. "Her doomed home" sounded sadder, and she wanted it all as sad as possible.

> from ~~the doomed house~~ *her doomed home*. At the top of the suitcase was a flat folder. In it were seven watercolour paintings and some half-done sketches. They were all of fruit and flowers and gardens; peaceful subjects from a peaceful time.

"No—*images*, not *subjects*," said Amber, and made the correction. correction.

flowers and gardens; peaceful ~~subjects~~ images from a peaceful time. Sighing, she laid them aside.

Hope flared briefly with the discovery of a small wooden box beneath the folder. It was a music box, but she didn't dare to wind it up. Small creaks and rustles from an empty stable wouldn't make the guards suspicious, but tinkling music certainly would! Wistfully, she wondered what tune it would play.

The mirrored lining of the box flashed as she opened it. Inside lay a small treasure of costume jewelry which had belonged to her grandmother. She let the fine chains and beads run through her fingers, pouring them from palm to palm like sand.

> Something soft brushed her knuckles — a velvet rose. She lifted it gently from its nest in the music box and held it against her cheek, wondering. The flower was crushed and faded, so why had her grandmother kept it so carefully? Had it been special? Had she worn it to a ball? Had it been an ornament on her first evening dress? Or in her hair?
>
> Holding the stem delicately between her finger and thumb, she rose from her cramped position on the stable floor. She stretched her cold muscles and moved silently away from the window, scuffing slightly through the hay. She paused for a moment and then raised the flower and laid it against her hair.
>
> Slowly, solemnly, she began to dance, waltzing to the music in her mind. Faster and faster she whirled, faster — until she sank down on the hay and sobbed silently, her shoulders shaking. The rose was still clenched in her hand. The cold winter sun dropped down and the dusk crept into the stable. Still she sat, unmoving, until full darkness came.
>
> Darkness. She sat up with a jerk, staring wildly around in the gloom. She staggered to her feet.
> It was time.

That was a good part, thought Amber approvingly. Plenty of contrasting emotions there. But what could it be time *for*? The big getaway? Hardly. The rest of the suitcase still had to be unpacked. Surely there'd be more in it than a folder and a music box.

When Amber and her sister, Kerry, had unpacked Gran's old case a few days before, there had been all sorts of stuff in it. Hey! How about using *all* the stuff out of Gran's case for the story? Amber nodded emphatically to herself. She liked that idea.

Now then. The fugitive would probably have to lie low until well after sunset. After midnight, even. Frowning, Amber decided on the darkest hour before dawn for the great escape. But there had to be some action right now. The girl couldn't just stay in suspended animation in the stable for the rest of the evening. One could, of course, indicate the passing of time with a row of asterisks, and take up the story again at midnight, but that was taking the easy way out. What could she do? What *would* she do? Sleep? Cry? Eat? With relief, Amber remembered the vegetable garden and the raw spinach. Supplies. It was time for a raid.

> Arms outstretched, she shuffled her way to the window, now a lighter patch in the featureless wall. From there she could trace her way by touch to the door. Fingers brushing the rough wood, she fumbled blindly along. At last! Her hand was resting on the cold iron bolt.
> She grasped the bolt carefully in her numb hands and slid it along in its socket. Cautiously, she swung the door open, and peered out. Nothing. Nothing but the cold night wind blowing bitterly across the yard. Nothing but the spinning leaves that mingled with the flying flakes of ash from many fires. She sniffed, and the smoke came rolling heavily towards her on the wind, carrying with it the unbearably tempting smell of roasting meat.

Would "they" be cooking on open fires? wondered Amber. Wouldn't "they" use the stove in the house "they" had just taken over? She shrugged. Probably the power lines were all down. Or else electricity hadn't reached this particular country yet.

Amber pondered, and opted for the second idea. This sort of invasion semed more fitted to an earlier time, anyway. Nowadays "they" would simply have pressed a button in some foreign capital city and KERBOOOOOM! no more house, no more stable, no more fugitive. No more anything, probably.

But maybe "they" weren't human.... Amber played with the idea of endowing "them" with purple ears and slimy green feelers, but she knew it wouldn't do. Certainly, it would be alarming to be invaded by such creatures, but for pure horror, what could beat being attacked by your own species?

And that led to another minor problem. Where were the other members of the fugitive's family? Should Amber have provided her with a relative or two? Not a parent, or the fugitive wouldn't have to make any decisions; but how about a younger brother or sister? It was a good idea, but the notion of rewriting all the pages already done didn't appeal. So where were the others?

Then a new idea struck Amber. The idea was so deliciously horrible that she sat perfectly still for a whole minute, while her apple core dropped unheeded on to the hay. What if — *WHAT IF* the rest of the family *were* the invaders? What if they had been taken over in some way and turned into monsters? Amber could see it all now. The fugitive having to run away from creatures who looked like her family on the outside, but who were really *them*.

Then she sighed reluctantly. She couldn't do it. Maybe some real genius of a writer could make that idea believable, but Amber Dale didn't have the talent. Yet. For now, the rest of the family would have to be "missing presumed dead." Something else to put in at the beginning of the story when she copied it out.

> She swallowed. There was no way she'd be able to steal any of that food that smelled so tempting. All she could hope for was some muddy plunder from the vegetable garden. Even raw cabbage seemed appetizing now. She had had nothing to eat since this morning.
>
> She crept out of the stable, leaving the door closed but unbolted. She crossed the yard, bent low and scurrying, mouse-like, in a grotesque parody of the games of hide-and-seek she used to play. And it was dark. Dark. Sometimes she stumbled, and the way to the garden seemed endless. If she could just get round behind the house... but what was that new sound coming on the wind? What was the source of that new sea of rolling smoke?
>
> She dropped to the ground, choking, and peered around her with wild, streaming eyes, staring in blank horror at the garden, now leaping with light and shrivelling with heat.

Amber read it over, and wondered if the writing was getting a bit hysterical. Then she crossed out "rolling" and substituted "roiling". She wasn't too sure what it meant, but it sounded good, and could be checked in the dictionary later.

> Like a marionette being pulled by strings, she rose to her feet and, shielding her face with her arms, watched as her home burned. Flames flared from the upper windows, licking out and leaping greedily into the trees.
> "I hate them!" she choked.

How ghastly! thought Amber with relish. How absolutely—horribly—entirely—ghastly! *Now* what? Could this possibly be the end? She went back and read through the closely written

pages, crossing out a word or two here and there, and adding others. Her fingers were cramped by now, and she hoped she had reached the end of the story. But she hadn't. There had to be more. Amber sighed, stretched her fingers, and slowly began to write.

> Suddenly there were figures outlined against the glare. Them. And it looked as if they were gloating. Off to the side was an uneven, jumbled heap. She squinted against the sharp shadows cast by the leaping flames.

Amber caught herself using a cliche, and crossed out "leaping."

> against the sharp shadows cast by the ~~leaping~~ flames. It was furniture from the house. They must have looted it before it burned. She quivered. And now another fire had sprung up in the darkness beyond the stable. She supposed it was the barn. She must go, and quickly, before one of them saw her standing there, caught like a moth between the two beacons of light. She must return to the stable.

Chilled with horror, she flitted across the open ground. She slipped back into the stable and cowered, panting, against the bolted door. It was unbearably dark. Slowly, she straightened, and felt her way back to where a red glow revealed the window. As her eyes became accustomed to the faint light, she made out a darker shadow on the floor. For a heart-stopping instant, she thought it was another human being, crouched in the hay, then her groping fingers met a sharp, angled edge. The suitcase. She had almost forgotten.

The light reflected from a mirror—it was the music box, still open on the ground. She took out the necklaces, one by one, and hung them around her neck, remembering her grandmother who had worn these things before her.

Head on one side, Amber considered the last part. *Would* the fugitive really mess around, trying on necklaces and things?

Maybe, if she was trying to forget her desperate situation. She glanced at her watch. She really ought to be getting in for dinner, before someone came looking for her. But she *had* to know what happened.

> Now that there was no chance of getting anything else from the house, the suitcase seemed more important than ever. Stretching out at random, her fingers closed around a silk scarf, cold and slippery. Fumbling, she tied it over her hair. Then came a limp-covered book — a notebook, by the feel.
>
> The lurid light was dying away from the window as the fires collapsed in on themselves. The thin sliver of a moon gave no more light than a firefly. She gave a sob of frustration as her fingers encountered a packet of wax candles. What use were they? Unless — she scrabbled frantically through the suitcase. There it was. A box of matches!

"Nonsense!" exclaimed Amber. "Nobody hides matches in suitcases—not even provident grannies!" The case she and Kerry had unpacked certainly hadn't had matches in it. Nor candles, for that matter. But why not? It made a wonderful little scene. Amber wished she could draw, so she could illustrate the story. What a touching picture it would be, when the match flared and lit up the white face of the fugitive, and steadied into a candle flame that illuminated—what?

> Her hands trembled so much that the first three matches broke without striking. She brushed some hay aside on the earthen floor, and dug a hole with her penknife so as to steady the candle when it was lit.

"Penknife?" wondered Amber, but it seemed like the right sort of thing for the fugitive to have, so she let her keep it.

> The last match flared, and sucked greedily at the wick. It wavered, then burned steadily. Crouching, she opened the notebook, but it was blank all the way through. Trembling with renewed anticipation, she turned her attention to the suitcase. All that was left was a layer of books, brown and dull, smelling of dust and age.
>
> She lifted out each volume in turn, tilting it to the candle so that she could read the worn gold lettering of the title. Only one was familiar — "The Secret Garden". The rest were long-forgotten books from eighty years before.

And *that* was all wrong, too, thought Amber. "The Secret Garden" probably wouldn't exist in the country where the fugitive lived. She crossed out the title. A pity, though, she thought. She always liked meeting book titles she knew in other books. It was like belonging to an exclusive club.

> She opened each book and read the affectionate messages on the fly-leaves. These had belonged to her grandmother. She wept, for her grandmother who was dead, and for herself, who was alive.
>
> She laid the books down gently. When it was time to run, she must run fast, and without looking back. She could take the jewelry, tied up inside the scarf, but everything else would have to be left. Even the candles were of no use without matches, and the matches were all used up. The suitcase was useless.

Good, approved Amber. Plenty of pathos and a really hopeless situation. Now for a really artistic ending.

> Her loneliness overwhelmed her then. She put both hands over her face and pressed, feeling the hard ridges of cheekbones and chin as if they belonged to a stranger. She stayed like that for a long time, until the candle guttered out.
>
> When the stable door was forced open by a heavily booted foot, she was almost relieved. No more waiting in the dark. She wouldn't have to run. She held the crumpled velvet rose against her chest and turned to face the sentry who had found her.

"So that's where you've gone!" said Kerry, wandering into the barn with her dog behind her. "What are you doing in here? It was dinner time half an hour ago."

"So why aren't you eating it?" asked Amber, putting the notebook casually behind her.

"I have. What've you got there?"

Amber thought of saying, "Wouldn't you like to know," but she was hungry, so she didn't bother. She just tucked her book under her arm and headed for the warmth of the kitchen. Amber slid into place to bolt down her rather cold meal, but she hardly noticed what she was eating, and even Kerry's loud off-key singing in the bathroom didn't disturb her thoughts.

She couldn't wait to return to her story. It was too late to go back to her den in the barn, so she had to finish it in her bedroom. Amber perched herself on her bed with the notebook on her lap, but somehow the ideas wouldn't come. She didn't need much more, she thought. Probably about half a page, but it had to be right.

"What's wrong with you?" asked Kerry, wandering in with a towel wrapped around her hair.

"I'm writing a story," said Amber.

"For school?"

"No, because I want to. I was sitting out in the barn and I had this wild idea—how would it be if I really had to stay hidden? I couldn't get rid of it, so I decided to write a story about someone who did."

Kerry settled down on the bed. "Go on," she said.

"It's about this girl," said Amber, "and some sort of invasion force has moved in and taken over her house."

"What's her name?" asked Kerry.

"She hasn't got one. Because she's really the only one in the story. Anyway, in her rush to get out of the house, all that she can find to take with her is this suitcase full of stuff—like the one of Gran's that we sorted out the other day.

"She hides in a stable, and while she's waiting for it to get dark enough to escape, she unpacks the suitcase. The rest of the story's about what she finds in it and how she feels about it and what she does.

"Oh, and then the invaders burn her house down and, right near the end, one of the sentries breaks down the door of the stable and discovers her."

"Then what?" asked Kerry.

"Well, I haven't really decided."
"Who rescues her, you mean?"
"Oh, she's not going to be *rescued*."
"But she's *got* to be rescued," objected Kerry. "Otherwise, it isn't a very good story."
"But some stories have sad endings."
"I mean... well, if she isn't rescued, all that hiding and

thinking's been for nothing. Useless. You've *got* to rescue her. Go on, write it now."

"How?" demanded Amber, but Kerry shrugged.

"It's your story," she said. "But you can read it to me when you finish."

Amber rather liked the idea of that. She thought she'd make it really dramatic, but she just grunted. Kerry stared at her, slowly rubbing her wet hair on the towel.

"Oh, go away and stop staring," said Amber, and Kerry did.

> She didn't know what she had expected—whether she would be killed immediately or taken prisoner. She stared at the sentry, and was astonished, even in her terror, to find that he was little older than she. He seemed to be surprised too, and stared back. But she was tired—tired of it all. "Well, come on then!" she said, with her voice sounding high and thin. "Get it over with!" To her further astonishment, the young sentry lifted his finger to his lips in an unmistakable gesture.
>
> "Why?" she mouthed. The sentry shook his head rapidly and then from the breast pocket of his uniform he removed the last thing she had expected: a faded, stained photograph.

But wouldn't he be carrying it around in a wallet or something? thought Amber. Or no—how about a locket? Since the picture was presumably of his girlfriend.

> ~~a faded, stained photograph~~ a gold locket. He pressed a catch and the locket sprang open to reveal a tiny portrait of a girl.
>
> "Your sweetheart?" she asked, and the boy smiled and nodded, before replacing the locket in his pocket.

Amber groaned. The last thing she wanted was funny rhymes! She crossed out the last three words.

> locket ~~in his pocket~~. Again signing for her to be silent, he took her by the arm and led her away— away from the smouldering ruins of her home, away from the dark huddles of men, away into the night.
> And then he let her go and walked rapidly back to his people.

Amber stretched and sighed. Then she called to Kerry, who must have been lurking just outside the door.

"Well?" said Kerry, fixing her bright eyes on the notebook. And Amber began to read.

"I'm glad he let her go," said Kerry when Amber had finished.

But Amber wasn't so sure. "Do you really think he would've?" she said doubtfully.

"Of course!" said Kerry. "He did!"

"But in real life?" persisted Amber.

"In real life," said Kerry, "none of it would have happened."

Amber sighed but she couldn't explain what she meant. Somehow the ending she had just written didn't seem to match the story. It was like a donkey wearing a horse's tail. When Kerry had gone out, she sat down to write a new ending.

> *And when the rescuers came there was nothing to tell the pathetic story but an old battered brown suitcase, a splintered door, and a velvet rose crushed among the hay.*

That was more what she had in mind before talking with Kerry, and it seemed to fit the story. Tragic and artistic. But still she frowned. What if Kerry was right? Not about the helpful enemy boy—she was sure *he* had been a mistake—but about the story having been all for nothing if the fugitive died.

Would it be a better idea if she somehow managed to get away by herself? Or even if she died trying to escape. Surely that would be better than having her just give up.

Amber shook her hair out of her eyes. "For goodness sake," she said aloud, "I've got this far. *Surely* I can write a decent ending!" She stared at the wall for some minutes, and then, suddenly, began to scribble. At last she flung down the pen. "I don't know how other people might have ended it," she said firmly, "but this is the way *I* think it should be."

When the stable door was forced open by a heavily booted foot, she was almost relieved. No more waiting in the dark. ~~She wouldn't have to run. She held the crumpled velvet rose against her chest and turned to face the sentry who had found her.~~ She dropped the rose in the hay and, springing past the startled sentry, she ran out into the open air, past the smouldering wreck of the barn, and away — away from her old life — into the dark.